PHILIDIOMS

And Other Thoughts
To Live and Laugh By

by Rudy Behrens

Illustrations by Marc Mallin

[handwritten inscription: Nancy, Enjoy! Rudy]

Publisher Todd Behrens

Copyright

Dedication

This book is dedicated to my grandson Dylan, who, like his father and grandfather, "likes to be *teached*".

About The Author

Mr. Behrens retired as Research Manager for a large chemical company. He is primary inventor on thirty patents, has spawned six commercially successful products, one, a blockbuster, winning him a national award. During his career, he has written and presented many technical papers.

Before his retirement, he became legally blind. Thanks to the Veterans Administration who provided him with training and equipment, he was able to get to one of his passions: writing - using a computer that talks to him. This time, his writing is about humor and common sense philosophy. Other books that he is working on are 'The Rainy Day Years Ahead' (about the U.S. economy); 'Too many Sundays' (flourishing in retirement) and 'The Earth Below, A View From Paradise' (what must be improved on earth to qualify as Utopia).

Another passion literally saved his life: playing the piano. He was a Hospital Corpsman in the U.S. Navy early in the Korean War. Out of his class of fifty Corpsman who were attached to the Marine Corps, eighteen were killed, many others were wounded. One Corpsman was pulled out because he played piano and could entertain at the base. His love for music and piano is still strong. He plays lyrical jazz specializing in the old standards. He has played at the Waldorf Astoria on Cole Porter's piano and was asked back. He still does gigs today for charity.

Acknowledgements

Special thanks to Jan Kardys, literary agent, founder of Unicorn Writers' Conferences who encouraged me to publish this book, describing it as "brilliant mind candy".

Thanks to my many victims who listened patiently to my banter and by their responses determined what went into the book and what went into the trash.

My victims include friends, relatives and virtually anyone who crossed my path especially at Western Connecticut State University, Danbury, Ct. Senior Center, The Lions Club of Danbury, Ct., the Veterans Health Administration Hospital at West Haven, Ct. and various supermarkets and stores.

I'm honored to have had James Lomuscio as editor of this book, except for Part entitled 'The Benediction (Religion)'. He is a professor of writing, has won awards for writing and has been with The New York Times for eleven years.

Marc Mallin's talent as illustrator and cartoonist speaks for itself.

Without my son, Todd, this book likely would not have been published. He put it all together and got it out there.

Finally, thanks to my grandson Dylan, teenage pre-pro golf student for being who you are. Keep it up.

Table of Contents

Introduction

This book is a collection of original philosophical statements, idioms and other forms of humor and rhetoric compiled over many years. *Philidioms* (new word) is a contraction of philosophical statements & idioms. These thoughts have been categorized into twelve subject areas (Parts; see the Table of Contents). The last four: 'Government and Politics', 'On the Job (The Private Sector)', 'Education' and 'The Benediction (Religion)' contain much satire.

The style of writing with satire is similar to a modern Mark Twain (1835-1910), except less folksy and more succinct. It is interesting that Mark Twain found fodder for satire of education in his day. Today, with the proof of mediocre education in the United States, critics are having a field day. Those readers with children in public schools should find this part of major interest. No criticism should be inferred for those good, dedicated teachers scattered throughout the country.

Some of the Part on Religion assumes the philosophy of an atheist. This section is not meant to convert anyone to atheism, rather to show what an atheist may think but would not dare say.

Government satire is and has been an acceptable form of entertainment since our government was formed in 1789. This Part intends to further the tradition. The best way to make it better is to get involved to vote the can-kickers out of office.

Finally, let us not forget the private sector depicted in the

Part entitled 'On the Job (The Private Sector)'. Sometimes ruthless, sometimes fair, management creates jobs and depending on how well they manage, can also destroy them.

Some Parts, for example, 'Down At the Senior Center' are best enjoyed by older readers. However, many other Parts including 'Common Sense Philosophy' may also appeal to the younger readers. On the other hand, it may conjure up some curiosity for the younger readers to find out what appeals to grandma or grandpa, especially the satirical Parts.

Bottom line, there is something of interest to those of all literate age groups.

PART 1

Common Sense Philosophy

Truth travels slowly. Unfortunately, it too often arrives too late.

_____

Some say that more is better. I think that better is more.

_____

Doing nothing is not what I do.

_____

He is wisest who deceives himself into thinking that he is happy.

_____

Getting there first is good in a race or on a quiz show, but in other matters in life, it's what you do after you get there that counts.

_____

Human nature should include human nurture.

_____

Knowledge is what we get from listening, observing and reading. Unfortunately, experience, at times, is what we get without listening or reading or observing.

My wealth is in inverse proportion to my perceived needs.

I believe in the adage that when being demeaned, turn the other cheek. After that however, be mean.

The good thing about a postage stamp is that it sticks to a job until it's done.

Tense is better than past tense. Controlled tension in a difficult situation could save the day, even your life.

A work ethic implies being driven, not chauffeured. Although, some who are driven end up being chauffeured.

It is better to hear it twice than to forget it once.

What is *writ* is not *fer-git*.

It takes more than looking out of the window once in a while to keep in touch with reality.

It's best to find out what something is worth before you pay for it. How simple is that? Do you know anyone who paid too much for a house?

A minute ago it was almost noon and now it is midnight: The attitude of a busy person and probably a happy one.

It doesn't help to be a self-starter unless you're also a finisher.

Do you know anyone with an attitude like this? "Don't tell me what to do, don't tell me what to say, because I am perfect, I was *bornded* that way."

The best way to know how to deal with people is to first know their motives; second, make sure you know their motives and third; if necessary, impugn their motives.

Heartburn: Better let your head direct you rather than your heart. Many times it takes your head to get you out of the trouble that your heart got you into.

Treat me better than I am and I will be better than I was.

Admirable goal is to strive for at least one inch less than infinity.

One of the most important drills in life is to differentiate fact from fiction. This endeavor should always start by asking the second question. The seller asks faith; the buyer must demand facts.

Too much verbal baloney can lead to indigestion of the brain.

If you don't have the facts, it's no fun listening to you.

The time to speak up is when you're being put down.

Life is dull. I think that it would be better if I had someone to hate. I've tried very hard, but I can't seem to come up with anybody. I know others who don't have any problem finding people to hate at all. Why can't I be like them?

To practice tolerance you must tolerate each other. Somehow it doesn't sound very friendly.

To get your argument off the ground your message must be down to earth.

The worst kind of ignorance is arrogant ignorance.

To say that there is no reason for any action is unreasonable. There is a reason for everything.

Unfortunately, some are careful not to let facts interfere with their decisions.

Lazy man's credo: Nothing ventured, nothing lost.

To me, year-end clearance means time to reduce inventory of stuff in the house that I likely will never need and may be appreciated by someone else. As someone so wisely wrote "It is better to use things and love people, than to love things and use people."

Poor is when all that you have left in life is your opinion
and no one is willing to listen to it.

You've heard 'if it ain't broke, don't fix it', but what I
would like to know is... if you're broke, who fixes you?

Be not the first by which the money is spent nor the last to
know where it went. Above all, make sure that you pay the
rent before you've spent your last cent.

The danger of using metaphors is that they sometimes
should more aptly be called *mythaphors*.

They either know or they don't want to know, so why tell
them?

It is better to have tongue in cheek than outside.

Some think that the argument which is the loudest is best. Actually, at high decibels, hearing is irritated and listening stops.

 Key requirements to be a victim of advertising is gullibility, blind faith and a line of easy credit.

The impossible dream from a major clutterer: "Give me a minute to get organized." I believe that this trait is inherent and cannot be cured.

Do not delight to debase, demean, defame, or deride. Rather, choose to debate.

It is better to follow up than to foul up.

If you are hammered (intoxicated) while driving, you are likely to be nailed (arrested) and sent to the 'big house' (prison). Not a good thing.

Why do tomorrow what you can avoid doing today?

The more knowledge that you amass as you age, the less anyone wants your advice.

Don't think outside the box for too long. There is a possibility that you may lose sight of the box.

In this world there are two kinds of people: exploiters and exploitees.

When an ordinarily friendly dog gets hit by a car, for example, it suddenly becomes vicious and distrustful of everyone. So with humans. A particularly bad experience can seriously destroy our trust in mankind (lawyers, politicians, doctors, bankers, stock brokers, salesmen, etc…). Best to trust <u>yourself</u> after doing your homework.

Ideas are especially precious to those who rarely get them. Beware of sterile chickens looking to roost on another's nest (idea piracy).

Trust must be earned not demanded.

What this world needs is a remote that works on people.
Just think about it. The mute button, volume control, and
best of all … the off button. Wow!

———————————

I used to be different. Now I'm indifferent.

———————————

How much money would you need if you had no mortgage on your home, had low real estate tax, kept your Japanese car for 20 years, food-shopped carefully and purchased home heating fuel when it was less expensive? Answer - Not much. With what you save you could travel around the world or otherwise live it up. If that's not where you are right now, at least you can make this your goal.

———————————

Those who live in the past have no future.

———————————

"You are an offense to those with common sense. Your pretense and arrogant ignorance is immense." You may want to use this on someone you think deserves it. Feel free to embellish it, but keep your cool.

———————————

Multi-tasking is better than no tasking.

When all are corrupt around you, the overwhelming temptation is to rationalize your way out of your integrity and join the crowd. Don't give in.

Those that work hard, work for those who work smart.

The greatest compliment is to be emulated.

A self-starter is a good thing; to have to be jump-started is not.

Mantra for doers: Do, Did, Done.

Trophy is better than atrophy.

You don't necessarily get what you pay for, but you will always get what you deserve. Do your homework.

The four great needs for human survival in descending order of importance are drink, food, sex and learning. Consider that anyone with a thirst for learning will have plenty of food for thought.

Before making a commitment with tradesmen, lawyers, bankers, insurance agents, brokers, salesmen, doctors, etc., ask the 2nd, 3rd, 4th and 5th questions. Their primary goal is to get as much money from you as they can. Don't be so trusting. However, when it is clear that you have found an honest and competent one, stay with him or her.

Confused and unproductive: "Just busy trying to get caught up. Don't know where to start. It's crazy." These are the words of a person whose transmission is busted. At least the wheels are not spinning. Of course they can't without a transmission. The answer? Pick a task. Start one step at a time until the job is finished. Then, encouraged by the knowledge that you have accomplished something, go to the next task. Before you know it, you have accomplished a lot and your excuses for being confused have vanished. You have proven that you could do it and can repeat the performance.

Scrooge's dilemma: The more we save beyond what in our lives we could ever spend, the more we waste since it is likely that our heirs will blow the bundle. Moral: money earned is appreciated money. It provides a sense of accomplishment.

One people-pleasure is to talk about the weather. I feel sorry for those who live in dull climates, that is, those without seasons each with its own pleasurable characteristics - winter, summer, spring and fall. For example, it's not boring to live in the Northeast.

It's tough to live by the adage 'Never park the Cadillac in front of the store' so as not to arouse the envy and jealousy of the customers. People tend to respect those they know are wealthy. Like Rodney Dangerfield, who claims to get no respect, those who hide their wealth for whatever reason, will suffer from a lack of an ego trip. Hey! That's OK. I'll stay that way.

To say you can, then you will. To say you can't, then you
won't. Simple isn't it?

Don't be judgmental unless you are a judge and get paid for
doing it. It will not make
you any friends but could create enemies.

Seeing may be believing, but listening is understanding.

'Gullible's travels' through life getting taken to the cleaners
at every turn. For example, advertisement junkies and
those who are nurtured by faith rather than facts.

Might makes right! No! Right makes Might. Maybe not on earth but it must be true somewhere out in the universe, don't you think?

If you think small, you are more likely to fall between the cracks in life.

Malapropism: Tongue depression (depressor). It is true that some tongue talk can be depressing to the listener.

"Look ma! Didn't I do good?" Remember when you needed encouragement and reinforcement? What can it cost you to boost someone's ego? It should be a joy.

It is said that 'the truth will make you free' but not until you have served your sentence. For the prisoner, the truth came too late.

Science adds to the quality and quantity of life. Fiction is only for entertainment or deception.

It's OK to run out of G.A.S. if it stands for Greed, Arrogance and Stupidity.

The genie often drank too much. One night while drinking
he got on the wrong side of the cork. It was then that he in
desperation to get out offered three wishes to anyone who
would pull the cork. Moral- Don't put yourself in a
compromising situation or you may have to give up the
store.

If you don't know what stupid is, then you likely won't care what brilliant is.

Misery likes company; happiness needs no one else.

What will you do after retiring as a truck farmer growing vegetables? I guess I will do what I know best, I'll just vegetate.

Leucocytes in our bodies protect us against infection. Would it not be great if we had something like *loonycytes* to protect us against irrational thoughts?

The world will end when you can't even trust the weatherman. Now he is an oasis of truth on television, a refreshing product of scientific thought.

Problem-prone people tend to perceive and persist in practices that produce plenty pain for themselves and others. Best to convert them to solution-prone people.

Debt is good until it's bad. Freedom from debt is a form of emancipation.

One of the most valuable properties that we humans have is integrity. It seems to be more prevalent among exploitees than exploiters.

Industries that depend for their businesses to thrive on arousing fear into their customers – religion, insurance, education, funeral and many manufacturers of products that involve safety and health. If dealing in these areas, knowing the odds will help you make the right decisions.

To seek is to find. To find is to have. To have is to share. To share is to love. (Catherine Scalise)

It is bad being under water with your house (owing more on your mortgage than the house is worth)? You don't hear anyone talking about being under water after you buy a car. You drive out of the show room with your new car, and you have already lost a lot of what you have committed to pay, enough to put many buyers underwater. Cars almost always depreciate, houses on the other hand generally appreciate.

What makes you happy?
- If your doctor tells you that you are healthy, you are happy.
- If you just got news that you landed a good job, you are happy.
- If you just met a promising person to share your life with, you are happy.
- If you just got word that you have been accepted to a college or trade school of your choice, you are happy.
- If you get better than expected grades on your tests, you are happy.
- if your team wins an important game, you are happy.
- If you just got good news on any subject, you are happy.
- And on and on…..THINK HAPPY

———————————

For some people the most difficult words to say are " you are right"

———————————

Push-ups are better than put-downs.

———————————

Civil society begins at home.

———————————

You don't get answers if you don't ask questions. Then you must assess the quality of the answers. It is most often better to ask too many questions than too few.

———————————

Were you using me as a sounding board or as a dart board?

———————————

Without clout you're out.

———————————

One door to success opens another, but only if your listening skills are good and you keep your eyes open and focused on your goal.

———————————

Most kids are eager to learn the truth. Why does society feed them with parables, myths and fables as if they were the truth. OK, maybe Santa Claus, but the rest?

_____

To a pessimist, good news is depressing.

_____

Ideas are especially precious to those who rarely get them. Beware of sterile chickens looking to roost on another's nest (idea piracy).

_____

To solve many problems in life, common sense is preferred over intelligence. Ideally, both would be helpful.

_____

PART 2

On Your Own Time Off

Above the naval base at San Diego is a tourist lookout complete with gift shop and telescopes where for a quarter you can see the naval base and surrounding San Diego sites. Trying to help the gift shop make it through the slow season, I suggested to the manager that they put a sign on some of the telescopes, fifty cents for spies.

———————————

On a trip to Egypt I learned that the Egyptians don't have any written vowels. I asked why? The tour guide said that in ancient times the Romans came and seized all. Now all the vowels are used by the Italians.

———————————

Since I have a photographic memory, I don't bother to take a camera.

———————————

Thinking about cameras, here's a camera ad I'd like to see: 'If you want to be a Big Shot, Buy a Canon.' Makes sense to me.

———————————

———————————————

Do you have GPS for your car? No, but we do have PHF.
What is that? That's my wife, the best pothole finder in the
business.

———————————————

Cry of a flat tire: 'Spare Me.'

———————————————

I'm not well traveled, but my luggage is thanks to my
airline.

———————————————

When going to Ireland you'll see a lot of castles and pubs.
In other words, old stone forts and old stoned farts.

———————————————

Vacationing at the Grand Canyon, I looked over the edge and thought this needs help so I put up a sign 'Fill Wanted Here'.

You play golf? Yes I do! I play in the 70's. That is very good! No! I just don't play if it's any colder than that.

If you are into feng shui, forget about decorating your house in early tag (garage) sale.

Oxymoron: written improvisation.

At Gettysburg, a young tour guide, in period costume on Main Street, the site of the most intense fighting during this Civil war battle, pointed to the home of Sally Ward. During the battle, Sally was sitting in her rocking chair on the front porch. She decided to go into the house. As she got out of her chair, a cannonball hit her chair and rent it asunder. I raised my hand to the young tour guide and asked, "Does this mean that sometimes it's OK to be off your rocker?"

Almost unbroken solitude: While sitting in a lawn chair on a terrace thirty steps above the waters of the Great Peconic Bay in eastern Long Island, just after Labor Day, I noticed an eerie silence later broken by the sound in the distance of an obviously amateur carpenter using his hammer. This vast space of earth, to be so quiet only an hour away from New York City, to me was astonishing. Such solitude you might only expect on a deserted Island or at some other uninhabited place somewhere on earth.

A tourist at the edge of the Mohave desert asked why this was a desert? The tour guide responded, " they didn't pay the water bill."

The Arts

Comedians are funny 'ha ha'; Poets are funny 'peculiar'. However, musicians are not funny at all (with rare exceptions). Music is meant to muse the myriad machinations of the mind.

───────────────

I got a standing ovation at my last concert. Why not! The audience had no seats. It was a concert in the park.

───────────────

Advice to budding composers - If you want to write colorful music, use the chromatic scale.

───────────────

The arts appeal to the senses. Science appeals to sense.
We need both.

———————————

Some violinists in the orchestra can't make it to first bass.

———————————

Lyrics help you to remember the tune. Music makes it memorable.

———————————

Talent is appreciated when advertised.

———————————

Drummers don't cuss, they percuss.

The power of music can, in the time of war, send men to the battlefield with high spirits and raise the morale of a nation.

Some jazz, the frenetic acrobatic kind, of all music is closest to sports. Not even those in marching bands get as much exercise during their performance. This music, although very difficult to play and very impressive, is not the kind of music that you can tap your feet or sing or dance to. This is probably why of all the music CDs sold in the U.S., it accounts for only about 3% of total sales. Impressive but to many, not entertaining.

It so far has eluded our politicians that there is no fee for poetic license. I won't tell them if you don't.

Not knowing that he was speaking to a famous pianist, he asked, "Do you play piano?" Modestly the pianist responded with, "Yes, I play a little piano. Well actually, I can also play a big one."

Good Sport

- Winter sports leave me cold.

- Kids are being groomed earlier and earlier these days for sports. Now they have baseball for little kids called T-ball. I wonder if their bases are called T-bags?

Gag Definition

- Loser: If at first you don't succeed, why try again?

- To overstaying guests: If at first you don't succeed, say bye, bye again.

- Lawyer's creed: If at first you don't succeed, lie, lie again and again and again.

- Egotistical musician: One who toots his own horn.

- *Chromatose*: One who doesn't know that he's color blind.

- *Pre-curser*: State of mind you're in just before you get angry.

Optimist: One who, on a fishing boat, when he sees a whale, yells out, "Quick! Get me a fishing pole."

If it came to that, I would sell my organs before I'd sell my piano.

I play the piano. Some one asked me why I play some songs with only one hand. I told them that I use only one hand for short songs. I can not see wasting my other hand on those.

I play piano. I play only passing tones because I'm always searching for the right note and don't get there on the first try.

Oxymorons

- Holy Hell

- Pretty Ugly

- Creative Non-Fiction (history books, auto-biographies, financial statements, political speeches, ads of all kinds, etc.)

- Passive Passion

- Taught to Play Piano by Ear

- Political Science

- Busy Sleeping

- Benevolent Bureaucrat

- Had a Miserable Merry Christmas

- The Big Nothing

- Large Minority

- Standard Improvisation

Other Thoughts

G.R.O.W. - Get Rid Of Waste

What did one exhausted cloud say to the other after the storm, when the thunder and lightning had passed and a ray of sunshine poked through the clouds? Answer - Breaking up is hard to do.

Legos are not in the realm of physical sports, but they are an endeavor that many kids and even some adults enjoy. A man went into a store to buy legos for himself. The salesman told him that there were two grades of legos, regular and very strong. The heavy duty kind withstands the weight of a man. The customer indicated that he wanted the heavy duty version. The salesman said that they were out of stock, and that right now they don't have a lego you can stand on.

How is boxing similar to soccer? In soccer you take it on the shin.

PART 3

Eating Can Be Healthy

My luck is so bad that I broke my tooth on a fortune cookie the other day. The saying inside read "You will soon be going on an unexpected trip." Yeah, to the dentist!

———————————

Unwritten sign at the local diner 'If at first you don't succeed, fry, fry again.'

———————————

I have found that you get your money's worth at the local diner. After you've eaten, you can still taste the food for hours.

———————————

The waitress at the diner was trying to be helpful. When asked to deliver a cup of coffee with half decaf and half regular, she sincerely asked "Which do you want on top?" True story.

———————————

For the best in Mexican food, try 'Jose's Too Hot to Holler Hacienda'.

Considering the dangers of junk food, you must either ration or rationalize.

My wife worries that I'm getting too fat. So now, when she shops at the supermarket, she buys items from the reduced section.

A shy woman, embarrassed by her excessive weight, was depressed one day. I told her that she was definitely not fat, only fluffy. She perked up.

Butter is marginal; margarine is a bit better. But better yet is neither. You could try olive oil.

Good vittles will help your vitals.

Diet Tip: To help reduce, try eating one nut at a time.

I approached the service desk counter at our supermarket and asked if it was true that the service desk area was to be divided into two sections, one for rain checks and one for snow jobs. They all laughed. That is why we still shop there.

On business one day I stopped for dinner before checking in at the hotel. Across the aisle from me was a woman also dining alone. I overheard her complaining to the waiter several times that it was either too hot or too cold in the restaurant. After she left and I was about to pay my bill, I asked the waiter, "How could you stand that woman? First it's too hot and then it's too cold." "No problem," he said, "We don't have air conditioning."

To vegetate may be good for the digestive system but it is a bummer for the brain.

My wife says to others that I have a drinking problem. After the sympathetic sighs and gasps simmer down, she explains that he doesn't drink enough water. To me it seems like a lifetime between her first and second comments.

Sign over a hot dog stand on the highway 'Burpo's Garlic
Hot Dogs. We enjoy repeat business.'

Big busted, big butted, bleached blonde bimbo parks her BMW in a handicapped spot in front of the supermarket. Since there was no physical evidence of handicap, I am left to presume that she must be mentally challenged. I feel badly for her, don't you?

One of the best comedy acts I've seen lately are wine experts, going through their antics, trying to convince the audience that what they're doing is legitimate and that they can actually pick out a good quality wine consistently. A few years ago three wine experts were given taste tests on just three wines. Result: No correlation.

A famous Jamaican Chinese chef stated that you must always serve the stir fry before the rum dish. He went on to explain that in any discipline you must first WOK before you rum.

Man in line in front of me at the coffee wagon remarked to the server, "What happened to the Danish?" I offered, "They changed their sex, now they are Swedish." He bought an apple strudel instead. You can't go wrong with that.

Today we honor Georgio, famous bread baker, teacher and ROLL model.

You can buy Llama meat in a NYC deli now (Peruvian). Eating 'Deli Llama' to me seems like a religious experience. Can't imagine why.

The world is getting smaller. It makes me feel guilty. I feel that just to continue to fit into it, I must go on a diet. How's that for inspiration?

My wife often says that she is trying to cook a meal. I have to admit that her meals are sometimes trying. Overall, she has a good batting average. I had to say that or she wouldn't let me publish this book.

Chuck steak is like a bad mortgage …sub prime.

We know that second hand smoke can be deadly. Does it follow that second hand garlic can be healthy?

Ever notice that French restaurants don't offer doggy bags. No surprise, they don't sell food, they sell presentation (the art of putting a little food on a plate in such a way that you admire it as a work of art and are reluctant to eat any of it for fear of sacrilege to an artist's work). The wine is good though.

In this world of half truths, a section on 'stupid questions and predictable answers' could start with asking the waiter, "Is the fish fresh?"

Some items at our supermarket have prices lower on the shelves than at the checkout counter. A good shopper can pick out a price discrepancy when the item is rung up by the cashier. They should take it to the customer service desk and, in accordance with state law (CT, NJ, NY), get the item for free. Check the law where you live.

What culture did we get from Tibet? Why, yogurt of course. Can't get any more cultured than that.

Nutritionists advocate eating lots of vegetables to keep slim or to help you lose weight. I don't know about that. Aren't Elephants vegetarians?

I have found that to be a well-rounded person you have to eat a lot of donuts. Just ask any cop.

I never thought that I was good enough to deserve angel food cake. What about you?

The more pick-me-ups that I eat, the more difficult it is to pick me up.

Shopping for food is putting your money where your mouth is.

The best rich is rich food, for example cheese cake. However, both money rich and food rich can be harmful long term.

Be careful how high you raise the bar. At some point you won't be able to reach your drink.

The supermarket chain Stop n' Shop just bought a chain of motels. They are going to call them Stop n' Flop.

The only optimists I know who see the glass as half empty are bartenders.

Difference between a sand bar and liquor bar. The sand bar leaves you high and dry. The liquor bar starts you dry and leave you high.

In Shakespeare's time, poor performance was rewarded by eggs being tossed at the performers. That was the beginning of 'Hamlet and eggs', now a breakfast staple.

Visiting a friend, I noticed a cookie jar shaped like a duck on her kitchen counter. I boldly asked what she put into it. Before she could answer I suggested that it would be good for *quackers*.

PART 4

Curious Creatures

She said her poodles Nicky and Pepe were almost human except for Nicky, when you take his dish away, he goes urh, urh. I said, "Well, to urh (err) is human."

Years ago there was a great Broadway show called "Cats." I heard someone say he couldn't get tickets for 'Cats'. I answered, "That's not surprising, you can't get tickets for dogs either."

Our neighbor down the street came to our door desperately looking for her lost cat, Meow. She said that Meow was very friendly and she couldn't understand why she would leave. In fact, she said that the neighbors on the left and right would feed her and even the neighbors across the street fed her. After hearing all that, it was clear to me why she left. She was just fed up.

Apparently a big concern that cats have today is that the world is going to the dogs. I understand that they believe that they should inherit at least half. They feel that because of their superior intelligence they could do a much better job. What do you think?

I'm told that Shakespeare had a dog named Spot. One morning, Shakespeare discovered that his dog had an accident on the rug. Upset, he threw open the door and shouted, "Out! Out! Damned Spot, life is but a passing shadow and you may be one soon." The rest is history.

It's sad when the faithful, devoted dog of the dear departed master is not in the master's will. It's tough especially for a dog to be left without a scent.

I try not to be early ever since I heard that the early bird catches the worm. I don't like worms. Never have.

Thinking about seagulls, last year it was so cold around here I saw a sea gull in the sky frozen solid. I told this to a woman I know who quickly demonstrated her shock on the plight of that poor bird. To her it was a grave situation when it should have aroused thoughts about gravity.

Gag definition: Dog conference - A bow wow pow wow.

Zebras, unlike horses, cannot be domesticated. It seems that they can't adjust to a new environment apparently because they've been behind bars too long.

What did the river say when it saw some beavers? "I'll be damned."

In the old movie 'The Fly', I could never understand why they chose to send out the army to kill the fly. It would have made more sense to send out the swat team.

I knew there was no chance for world peace after I saw two doves fighting.

A birds eye view depends on whether you're a vulture or an eagle or an owl.

_____

Never look a gift horse in the mouth unless you're a dentist.

_____

Where do bookworms eat? Answer: Wherever there's food for thought.

_____

I bought my turtle sneakers so he could get to his food before it got cold. I told this to a friend who suggested that I give him roller skates. Tried it, didn't work. He got there so fast that he burned his tongue.

Owls make wonderful mothers. They give a hoot…

If it were a dog-eat-dog world, would Chihuahuas not be extinct?

I went to a store to buy bird seed. The salesman asked me "What kind do you want?". I said that I asked the birds in my neighborhood and all I got out of them was "cheep, cheep… cheep, cheep. I guess that I want cheap bird seed. The price turned out to be nothing to crow about.

Waiting outside the VA doctor's office, I swore I heard a lion's roar. I wondered how he got to be a veteran. The doctor told the lion that he was ordering a blood test. He told the lion to fast for 24 hours before the test and and that he mustn't drink anything or eat anybody.

PART 5

People

How good are friends who visit you overnight on their way to a final destination and the only other contact is a Christmas card? They may have saved a motel bill but at least they stopped to visit.

───────────────

My wife and I visited a young friend in the hospital who just had a baby. My wife went to the mother's room and I went to the nursery to check out the newborn. As I approached the window where you could see the little ones, I thought that I heard, apart from the usual screaming and hollering, some talking from the loudspeaker above the window. Sure enough, when I got there I saw one guy turned in the direction of the little newborn next to him. He said, "You're new here aren't you?" The other little guy, apparently insulted by this stupid remark, replied "What! Do you think I was born yesterday?"

───────────────

One plus one equals four when you have twins.

───────────────

Teen pregnancy: From here to maternity.

Picture this: Three infant boys in clean white diapers sitting on a linoleum floor and waving their arms around aimlessly. The caption under this picture reads, 'The Soggy Bottom Boys' or translated into Japanese, 'The Mushie Tushie'. What better an ad for a diaper company?

Out of the mouths of babes oft comes drool.

Husband who didn't want children was asked by his pregnant wife, "What should we call the baby?" He callously replied, "Let's call it quits".

Credo of a spoiled child: If at first you don't succeed cry, cry and cry again.

Heredity is a major factor in determining actions of an individual. For example, a philanderer's problem is definitely in his jeans.

With men, the more beautiful the dress on his wife, the more he wishes it wasn't there.

A reporter for the Hartford Courant back in the 1880's asked Mark Twain whether his family would have a reunion. Mark Twain answered, "No! Ne'r the Twains shall meet".

To temper your Happy Holidays, think of the poor hermit who brightens his table with a pine branch, a candle and his only card, the one from the Electric Company.

Passed by a gay and lesbian picnic at the University last month. It reminded me of my junior high school dance; boys on one side, girls on the other, with one embarrassed kid dancing with a teacher.

I believe in monogamy, that is, one woman at a time.

No question. Weddings are so much fun. People should have several of them.

Advise to young marrieds looking for a house. If you want your marriage to last, buy a house with at least two levels. As you get older, the greater need for privacy and exercise will enhance your compatibility and life spans.

For years everything I said to my wife seemed to go over her head. At one point I felt it was beneath me to even talk to her. Then one day I finally figured it out, she's only five feet tall and I'm six feet tall. I now just talk down to her and all's well.

My wife gets her housework done during the TV ads. Thankfully, there are a lot of ads on TV these days or the house, I fear, would be a mess.

One morning I came up for breakfast and my wife, in a moment of weakness hugged me, looked up at me (she's five foot tall and I'm six foot tall) and said, "I think I'm getting shorter". I disagreed with her, "No, I think I'm getting taller. But I guess that in either case we're drifting apart at least vertically. Had a great breakfast.

My wife was on the phone so long one time that her ear got hoarse.

"Those aren't my shoes under the table, are they?"
"No! They're mine." "Those aren't my clothes on the chair, are they?"
"No! They're mine." "Shall I do the dishes?"
"No! I'll get to it later sometime." "I'm sorry I guess I'm too neat."
"No, it's just that I'm too beat." "But dear, this is routine."
"Maybe, but isn't it fun to evolve chaos out of order?"

"Let's call her." "Don't bother, she may not be home."
"But she may be home and it's a local call, so what's to lose?"
"OK! Go ahead, if you want to waste your time."
"Hello Cindy, You're there. Great! I would have called you earlier, but we had a little discussion going on here." Note: do you know anyone like this?

Happy Mud-der's Day!

Picture this: A Mother's Day card showing a little boy in
diapers sitting in a mud puddle and smeared with mud and
looking as happy as a pig in mud. To the side is his mother,
hands on her hips, with an exasperated look. The caption
under the picture reads: HAPPY MUD-DERS-DAY.

As we were driving along, my wife asked me if I was thirsty. I said "No. Why do you ask?" She came back with "I just saw a sign 'Liquidation Sale'. I thought that we should stop."

On rainy days my wife is depressed and virtually gets nothing done around the house. On sunny days, she gets twice as much done.

My wife complained to the doctor that she had a chronic pain in the neck. She came home with bad news. She told me that the doctor said to get a divorce.

My wife takes so long to get a meal on the table, that by the time it gets there, it's leftovers.

My wife buys all of my clothes. I can't be bothered. Last week she bought me what she called a gender defining pair of short pants. Then she warned me to wear them only around the house and not in public. Go figure.

Pedro and Jose were conversing in Spanish. Jose ended the conversation with "Si". An American friend asked Jose, "What did Pedro say?" Jose answered, "He wanted to know what comes after B."

Now I know why it's called a remote for the TV. I have a good one. It's so remote that I can't find it.

Example of give and take: Either you give it to me or I will take it from you.

I thought that we were incompatible until I got to know her. Only then did I come to realize why, but by then, we were already married.

An optimistic driver in a traffic jam, said to his wife after coming to a stop, "well, at least we're not slowing down anymore."

One day our electric power went out in our house: no radio and no television and no computer. It was then that I realized that I had completely forgotten how to talk to my wife. We grunted at each other for a while, but soon some complete sentences started to come out and in a few hours we actually had a reasonably normal conversation, so much for high tech.

Like all relationships, sometimes they're OK and sometimes they're not. For example last week we were on the outs. I was so discouraged that I told a friend how bad I felt. I'm thankful to him for his good advice. He said it's cheaper to keep her. With that incentive, I felt much better.

Egocentric people have trouble counting past one.

In the entertainment business they have several prestigious awards: the Oscar, the Grammy and the Tony. A more appropriate award for those in the land of make-believe would be the Phony award.

My wife told me that, sometimes when my mouth opens, my brain shuts off. Why do you suppose that is? Ah! I know the answer. It's when I go to sleep. Let's leave it at that.

My wife and I are on the 'outs'. Don't know what I did, but I hope it doesn't last long. I'm getting hungry.

A shy high school boy passed a note to a girl which read "If you like me, as I pass you in the hall next time, say 'chicken'." The next day she passed him a note which read "I couldn't do it. I was chicken."

If it isn't going, it needs towing.

The only thing that my wife finishes is my sentences and, to be fair, maybe a few other things.

New modern fashions in Turkey: The burkha bikini. How's that for an oxymoron?

When I first met my future wife, I said to her, "I'm now sure that there must be a God because, looking at and listening to you, I'm convinced that you came from Heaven."

Are you invited to a wedding because you are a good friend of the bride or groom's family, or because you have a reputation of giving an expensive gift or a lot of money? True test is after the kids are married off, how much contact do you then have with the families?

Wife called the doctor for her sick husband. The doctor told her to give him plenty of juice. She plugged him in. He got a charge out of it. He will never give her static again. At the trial, she claimed that she followed the doctor's directions. You can visit her in state prison.

Telephoned my mother-in-law a while ago on April fools day. Started with "Mrs. Petrie, Itsa my pleasure to informa you dat you almosta won two million euros in the Italian sweepastakes, We don'ta need your address because we got no money to senda you." My mother–in–law, wise to me, replied in her cute Italian accent " Atsa all right, I don'ta have any money to send to you either. Atsa no nice you shake a me up".

81

My wife derives great pleasure from food shopping. Sometimes she'll take me along kicking and screaming. We no sooner walk into the store when she hands me three store coupons for free items. I think she does this just to get rid of me. Since I am legally blind, I need help to find the aisle for the first item and in the aisle some kind lady helps me find the item. Sometimes, some of the women will even give me a recipe for the product they have just found for me (unsolicited). After I've completed my assignment, now I have a bigger problem, finding my wife. One time, a woman who had just helped me, approached me and said, "You look confused. What's the matter?" I answered, "If I don't find my wife in five minutes, I've got a major problem. Then I've got to go out and look for another one and I don't want to go through that again". She was a good sport and asked, "How long we have been married?" I told her and she came back with, "Well, for all that time you ought to give her twenty minutes anyway". I agreed. Fortunately, I found my wife in fewer than twenty minutes.

It took so long to go to the bathroom at a crowded wedding reception that by the time I got back to my seat, they were celebrating their anniversary.

Forget cosmetics! To me, the most beautiful sight on earth is a woman's smile. Told this to my wife who said "what if she has bad teeth?" With that pin, my balloon popped. Come to think of it, I wonder what Mona Lisa's teeth were like? There were no teeth showing through her smile. Ever notice? So much for that romantic thought.

I have bad eyesight. I'm afraid to go into a crowd for fear of getting lost. I solved that problem. Now I wear bright red pants. If I think that I may be lost, I just look down, see my red pants and know just where I am. Smart. No?

I'm so bald that when I go to my barber he takes one look at me and says hello and goodbye in the same sentence.

Oxymoron: Interior decorator for a compulsive hoarder.

My family would rather nit-pick than picnic. What about yours?

I have to be a good guy in life because I can't handle hot climates, especially anything as hot as hell. I am determined not to go there.

My girlfriend says that she wants to get married. I told her to go ahead and if it didn't work out she could come back to me. Label me a confirmed bachelor.

Statement by a compulsive hoarder in denial: " Everything in my house is neatly cluttered."

Wife to husband, "Did you hear what I just said?"
Husband replies, "Yes, but would you repeat the last few sentences just for emphasis?"

My wife and I share about everything. For example, when I talk to someone, I get to say the first half of the sentence and she finishes the rest. Isn't that great! I know some guys who can't get a word in edgewise.

My umbrella doesn't work. I brought it with me the other day and it rained anyway.

You can live with a lot of people, but there is only one that you can't live without.

How do you know when your wife really wants an answer to her question? Beats me! I've never figured it out after 50 years of marriage.

Ever since the Doctor cured my wife's 'trigger finger', I fear for my life.

Do you know anyone who asks you where something is before they start looking for it themselves?

I call my wife mushroom because you never know where she's going to pop up next.

My wife and I can't stand each other, but we're OK sitting down. This is probably true because I'm six feet tall and she's only five feet tall. We get stiff necks talking to each other, looking up and down.

I paged my wife, Maria, in a Spanish supermarket. Eleven Maria's showed up. Two of them wanted to marry me. I guess I was dressed up that day.

Many people like recycled plastic bottles. They like to be fleeced. Plastic bottles are composed of polybutylene terephthalate which is reprocessed and converted to fabric called fleece.

Sometimes married couples argue over money. You would think that the wealthy would argue more because they have more of it. Poor couples only have to argue over how to get more of it. Which is worse? It's probably worse for the rich since they can afford to get lawyers involved who will take away as much money as they can get away with.

We have the ideal marriage. We stick together through thick and thin. I am thick. She is thin.

Happiness is relative except for my mother in law.

Everything is relative, ask Einstein.

In the company of others who are good listeners, who talks?

Raised during the great depression, we were so poor that I had to rent a pair of shoes to go to my high school graduation. That was bad enough, but it took me a year to pay it off.

To some people low vision is when you are looking for your eyeglasses and you have them on.

I lead an exciting life. Every night I sleep with a strange woman (my wife).

I talked to a pretty, young woman in a department store for about 20 minutes before I realized that she was a manikin. I should have known that something was wrong because she seemed to agree with everything I said. I guess that I need new eyeglasses.

Since my eyes have failed me, I can no longer bait my fishhooks. My wife is very understanding and arranged for a hooker to help me when I go fishing. I go fishing a lot now. Happy days are here again.

Question to the officers of a veteran's organization: "If I move to another state, will I be dismembered?" Answer: "Only if you don't pay your dues".

PART 6

My Doctor Is Better Than Yours

I need to consult a doctor with common sense, who's experienced, intelligent and who will not run you over on the way to the bank. Do you know anyone like that?

I decided to sell my exercise bike after a long period of no use. My ad read, "Exercise bike for sale. Low mileage."

Drug company credo: The drug that works best is the one most advertised.

The guru says meditate, the doctor says medicate and the lawyer says mediate. The lawyer's right. The patient's food poisoning was from the *meat he ate.*

Good patient / doctor relationship: Doctor's life style depends on it. Patient's life depends on it.

Too many doctors suffer from greed, their worst occupational disease: They're afraid of being sued. They'll order too many tests from businesses they own. Thankfully, not all doctors are like this. It's sometimes difficult to tell them apart. You may have to shop around.

Mr. Payne complained to the doctor of a persistent backache. The doctor examined him, told him to take aspirin four times a day and to change his name.

Short of breath in bed for a week thinking I had a cold, my wife came to the bed to check up on me asking "Are you all right?" Poking my head through the covers, I weakly answered with the song 'So Long, It's Been Good to Know You.' I learned that afternoon how appropriate that song was when I went to the doctor. His diagnosis: life threatening pneumothorax or collapsed lung. After five days in the hospital, I was as good as new. Moral: Sometimes it's all right to get a checkup.

She claims that she has a cold, but I think it is all in her head.

Medicare Part D encourages drug use. It tells doctors to prescribe more medications than needed. Another gem from Congress.

A doctor I know studied abroad so long that he became a gynecologist.

You've been around you longer than anyone else. So, if you've been paying attention, you have the best chance of keeping yourself alive. Help well-meaning doctors to honor the most important tenet in their Hippocratic oath 'do no harm.' Ask a lot of questions. Doctors are fallible.

A friend of mine is a gastroenterologist. His name is Hooper. His calling card has on it a drawing of the backside of a skunk with his tail in the air. Under this, it reads, "Dr. Hooper, Super Duper Pooper Scooper". With a job like that I guess you need a good sense of humor. True story.

Speaking of Dr. Hooper, turns out he knows Dr. Cleaver. You know what I'm about to say. I'll say it anyway. Yes! He's a retired orthopedic surgeon specializing in amputations. Enough said. Again, true.

Ever think about the expression "God bless you" after someone sneezes? It seems more appropriate to say "God help us." After all, the sneezer's spreading germs.

Hygiene lesson: Never use a stranger's comb, cause little cooties like to roam.

Cold climates are like refrigerators. Perishables last longer in a refrigerator. Perhaps that is one reason why people live longer in colder climates. Check it out.

Healthy is a good thing. It's high on the list of topics of conversations. Yet for many it can be overdone. My 97-year-old aunt would discourage such conversations by saying "What's the big deal? Some people have this and some have that. Everybody's got something."

When you are healthy, your age is just a number. It's when you are ill that the number takes on significance.

A manifestation of the 'do no harm' part of the doctor's Hippocratic oath - "Doctor , are you sure that this medicine will help me? Doctor answerers "Well it can't hurt. How is that as a confidence builder?

What we need in the world is more evidence-based
medicine. Evidence should be a result of solid science.
Nutrition, unfortunately, too often falls into the realm of a
pseudo science replete with pronouncements of fact based
on flimsy or even no evidence. Much misinformation
comes from manufacturers eager to sell their products.
The gullible literally eat them up.

Does it matter when you have a cold whether or not you go
to the doctor? Not really. In either case you pay through
the nose.

PART 7

Down At The Senior Center

At a mansion in Newport, RI, young actors in period costumes were applying their craft. In a large ballroom, a young lady asked me to dance. I accepted the challenge. While dancing, she remarked, "I just graduated from finishing school." "What a coincidence," I said, "I just graduated from refinishing school."

———————————

I'm so old, I prefer the before picture in the exercise ads.

———————————

Difference between young and old people: Young people wanna party whereas old people would rather potty.

———————————

A school bus full of senior citizens was passing through a construction zone. Pat and Mike, policemen directing traffic looked at those in the bus and remarked, "Those school kids look pretty old. They must have been stuck in traffic a long time!"

———————————

I am reluctant to visit someone in psychiatric hospitals or even assisted living institutions for fear that they won't let me out.

You know you're old when no one sits next to you on a crowded train.

An old man was cozying up to an old lady at the senior center one day after lunch. The old lady said to the old man "If you get any closer, it'll cost you!" No man with a cane has ever moved away from a woman so fast.

It's not surprising that older people tend to be forgetful, after all they have a bigger inventory of knowledge and memories to recall.

As I get older, some of my most used parts are beginning to wear out. On that basis, my brain should hold up for a long time to come.

Gag definition: Face of an octogenarian man - Octopus..
You take it from here.

Being old is not so bad. I get lifetime subscriptions and
club memberships much cheaper.

Why is it that some people are so disposed never to appear
young, while others though physically old, never appear to
be so? Attitude! That's it!

Went across the street to say hello to my 92-year-old
neighbor, Henry, who was sitting in his rocking chair
drinking beer. I noticed his cap read 'Hot Stuff.' He said
that some young ladies bought the hat to cover his bald
head. After settling down with small talk, I asked how his
93-year-old wife was. His answer was "Oh, she's no fun
anymore."

You know you're old when you start to play tennis, get ready to serve and you notice vultures circling above.

Senior center: Country club without a golf course or docks with yachts. However it does have Wii bowling and some of the same kind of cars (Lexus and Mercedes) in the parking lot.

When you start looking like a prune, it's then that you need them.

I suffer from A.A. (Advanced Age). Well, actually I don't really suffer much yet. I am only 85 years old.

Picture this: An ambulance waiting with stretcher ready at the exit doorway to a senior citizen's dance. What a way to go!

PART 8

The Grand Finale

Crematorium ad: We make money the old-fashioned way. We urn it.

A good thing about deflation is that you can live longer. Think about it. The longer that you live, the cheaper it is to die with prices going down. What greater incentive do you need?

Have you heard what a funeral costs today? I think I'll wait for one of those drop-dead sales.

You know you won't be around much longer when you notice that the doctor put your name on his records in pencil.

A famous person once said "It's a bad year to die. Too much competition."

Making your funeral arrangements is like studying for your finals.

Since more people are being cremated these days, it is not hard to understand that even funeral directors must think outside the box.

Who is in the tomb shouldn't always be taken for Grant. Look what happened to Lincoln.

You're in a hearse only once. This is the one event in life that you can't re-hearse.

Molly Goldberg, looking into the coffin of her dear departed friend Gertrude, started talking to her. "Gerti, you look terrific. I see you're wearing your favorite dress. But me, I'm a mess! I got problems you shouldn't hear but I'll tell you anyway. My arthritis and gout are acting up again. My son Michael says he's divorcing his wife Leah and wants to live with us again. They can't sell their house or make payments on their Mercedes. My Irving is afraid he's going to lose his job. My sister Shirley had an accident with her car yesterday and is in the hospital. The rest I won't tell you so you shouldn't get depressed. Yes Gerti, you look good."

My friend's wife believed in reincarnation. For some reason she wanted to come back as a bee. Poor woman got sick and died. It was summer when, standing next to my friend at the cemetery service, a bee landed on his forearm. He looked closer at the bee and whispered " Agnes is that You?" Just then, the bee stung him hard. He then shouted " Agnes, it is You!"

When you are alive, they sign you up. When you are dead, they write you off.

Death is absence of thought. Do you know any living zombies? On the other hand, if your life is more positive than negative, life is a better option.

It's not fair. All of my life I took pride in being on time. Since I died, the angels tell me that I'm now referred to on earth as the late Harry Jones. The only thing I ever wanted to be late for was dying.

They say the good die young. I am 102 years old. Every time I wake up, I feel guilty. I can not understand. What did I do to deserve this?

I have no interest in reading the obituary column in the newspapers. If I found my name in one of them, it would just make me feel depressed, especially if they spelled my name wrong.

PART 9

Government and Politics

For the Ship of State to move forward in the treacherous seas of world competition, the United States must be balanced, with a similar number of those leaning left and those leaning right, lest the ship capsize.

As the government balloons in size compared to the private sector and, in the light of the private sector's growing animosity and resentment against government, we are heading into the growing probability of a civil war in the U.S.. Although different from the first, it will nevertheless be nasty.

China is an 'Authoritarian Capitalistic' country run by engineers. The United States is a 'Democratic Capitalistic' country run by lawyers. If you were asked to bet which one would win the race for number one super power, where would you put your money, on AC or DC?

Japan and Israel have decided to form a common currency. They will call it the yentl.

We call the head of local government in Connecticut first selectman. What do you call yours in New Jersey? We call them crooks.

Grand Cayman Islands: Where you can either 'Stay to Play' or 'Stash your Cash and Dash'.

The saying 'the government that governs least, governs best' should have a corollary; namely, 'the least of men should not govern'.

Following the vote at a controversial town meeting, the town clerk announced "Those of you who voted no and need a ride home, can still find some brooms left from the last meeting."

Every so often there is a drive by atheist organizations to remove 'In God We Trust' from our currency. I would suggest that, if the change is imminent, replace it with the statement 'Whatever sells.' Think about it. Isn't that the dominant theme of business in the U.S.? It doesn't have to be good or needed, it just has to sell.

We're taught that Democracies don't war against each other. If other countries had a Congress like ours, I could understand why. By the time Congress finishes debating about going to war, they have forgotten why they wanted to go in the first place.

At a reunion, I saw a classmate who, in school, was very politically active. He was then a staunch Republican. I asked him if he pursued a career in politics and was he still a Republican? He answered "Yes and no! I'm the mayor of my city, but I have turned Democrat. I couldn't get elected as a Republican." So much for principle. True story.

The 'Ins and Outs' of politics: What's 'In' it for me and what do I get 'Out' of it.

Politicians oppose human cloning. Maybe they fear a more intelligent electorate.

It is too bad that those articulate orators, debaters, politicians and lawyers who impress their audiences with magnificence, don't let the whole truth get in the way of their art or goal.

Ever notice that there are no action points resulting from round table discussions. Is this because no one is at the head of the table?

I believe it's a good idea to combine the Departments of Education and Energy. It would be synergistic. Lord knows, the Department of Energy lacks education and the Department of Education lacks energy.

Ever wonder why in days of yore that kings were so ready to go to war? It reduced unemployment, created jobs, reduced population and of course the boys in the army were often paid by pillaging. The king would be less likely to be murdered in his bed with the young Turks out of town. Thank goodness some things are different today. We still have pillaging by Wall Street and bankers and politicians of the assets of millions of U.S. citizens. It hurts when the pillagers walk away with hundreds of millions of dollars and then are rewarded by Congress by giving them the job to straighten out the mess they created. Whatever happened to the guillotine?

Where would the world be without economists? Answer: About the same. So far, most have acted as historians who think they have the answer on how to direct our economic future from previous economists' failed theories. Perhaps some day enough data will be generated to prove one of these theories correct.

Government workers should appreciate the sacrifice made by private sector employees. After all, on average, the first five months of their salaries goes to them each year in taxes.

Trouble with the two-party system is that the principles of the members of the parties are embedded in the party right or wrong. It's almost the rule that you compromise your principles to preserve the party. It is refreshing once in a while that you're faced with a party pooper. Now the party of the party pooper has to deal with the other party who doesn't have a pooper which could be an advantage or a disadvantage depending on the situation. Well, I could elaborate further, but I'm sure you've got the picture. Sounds like a lot of poop to me. Then there's the flip flopper. They are the worst, especially the flippant flip flopper. They arrogantly speak before they've done their homework. Somewhere along the way they find that they are wrong and they flop. Hopefully, they will flop in their next attempt at re-election.

We're familiar with the social sciences, but do you know about the anti-social science: political science?

Rousing the restless rabble may result in revolution in Russia, but then again, it may not. Give people a chance for a good life and insurrection will cease. How obvious is that?

Fixed pensions first introduced in Japan in the late 1800's, were set to kick in at age 55, just two years longer than the average life expectancy of the day (53 years old). Very shrewd of management. In the U.S. today, pension plans are being phased out and in some cases are replaced with 401K plans which fluctuate with the stock market. Are managements doing us a favor here? The best would be to have pensions that are indexed to inflation. However, this would not be in management's interest and for most businesses, it will not happen.

They say that opposites attract. It works in electricity, why doesn't it work in Congress? In Congress we do get a lot of static, but then again, no spark.

Global warming has become a political football. At least with global warming, you are sure that a rising tide will lift all boats.

A long-standing resolution in Congress tends to develop flat feet.

Perhaps because many people have lost their houses, the Democrats have also lost their house in Congress. They still have an edge in the Senate, but for how long? Then it will again be the Republicans turn to screw up. Won't the voters ever learn?

The President's plan to cut spending is good. He doesn't have to worry about reducing the number of his speeches because talk is cheap and should not contribute to the budget deficit.

Back in the first half of the 20th Century, Presidents were damned. For example: Wilson, Roosevelt, Coolidge and Hoover dams. Can you name any others? We can thank the depression for all of these infrastructure projects.

Congressmen have an approval rating today of only 13%. I thought they would feel badly about that but when I asked one, he said it didn't bother him at all because it was an improvement of 11% when he practiced law.

Test results for Congress: 'A' for oration, 'F' for convincibility.

Politically, centrists don't get run over on the road to the White House. They carefully avoid getting hit by traffic on the left or the right.

Why is it that every time I hear a politician talking about change, I think of diapers. Oh yes! Now I know why.

What does it say about voters when, invariably, the candidate who spends the most money wins?

_____

It is better to claim to be a reformer before you get caught.

_____

Public employees who disagree with their bosses may get fired, but in dictatorships, they get fired upon. Even in democracies there is a limit to freedom, but at least you get to disagree another day.

_____

The question is, is it a "robust" economy or is it just a "bust" economy?

_____

In the 2010-11 women's NCAA basketball season, Baylor had a 6'8" player who was too big to fail. She did it without a Federal bailout. We need more like that.

_____

YES ✔
NO ☐

The economy was so bad that Congress passed a law to cut out one of the 12 days of Christmas. I sent them an urgent e-mail and suggested that they keep the '8 maids a milkin' and remove the '9 lords a leapin'. I haven't heard back yet.

YES ☐
NO ✔

It seems ironic to me. Liberals believe in abortion and are against the death penalty. Does that mean that they think it is OK to kill an innocent baby, but it is bad to kill a serial killer.

Which is worse, kicking the can down the road or opening a can of worms. The former is for cowards; the latter is for the brave, especially when it comes to re-election.

Politicians, to be elected, must know what fertilizer to use to nurture grass roots.

I believe that the government should adopt a hands off policy, especially, hands off my wallet.

People who gave money away during the depression knew that their money was actually saving lives. Today, it's much less rewarding to give money away because the U.S. population now has a much higher 'stuff' level. As the economy deteriorates with all of the government entitlement programs, poor people will not starve or have their electricity turned off. They will still have television, cars, cell phones and other comforts that did not exist during the depression.

In war, glory soon turns to gory. Our President and Congress need to be more involved in the gory part. Perhaps, then the wars would be fewer and shorter.

Boris Yeltsin, former leader of the Soviet Union, was an alcoholic. Sculptures of him are all made in plaster, fittingly so, because he was plastered in life as in death.

Some people get hooked on entitlements so much that they are always on the dole. I feel badly for them. It must be boring living on pineapple juice.

In world politics, we took down the 'Iron Curtain' (the Soviet Union's tension against the U.S.) with our 'Rust Belt' (U.S. industrial might) resulting in the former's implosion. When the dust settled, only Russia was left and the U.S. stood like a beacon on the hill.

I was against the bill until I learned that the majority of those in the other party was also against it, so I voted for it. NO party pooper here.

Investigating reporters were once our heroes. They would expose bad happenings that affected the citizens. Now they are investigating other job opportunities. Many government agencies are doing a poor job at regulating and enforcing the law. What will happen to us now? We only have a few brave whistleblowers who are being attacked by government and corporations.

In good times, the government spends a lot. In bad times, they spend even more of our money (stimulus) to induce us to spend more. The result is extreme debt. The deeper the debt hole we dig, the more difficult it is to get out of the hole.

It's the political campaign season, or as I call it, the poly-sci-fi season.

It's not so bad that we have a do nothing Congress, but it is aggravating that now they
spend so much more of our taxpayer dollars doing it.

Too many politicians first run for some office. After elected they first run from office responsibility.

Politicians should have their hand on the tiller, to guide us on the path to a better life and not have their hand in the till.

Buddhists believe that everything is in a state of flux. I guess they do not know about the U.S. Congress. Nothing seems to change there.

Congress gets paid very well for what they don't do.

PART **10**

On The Job (The Private Sector)

A man who rises fast in the business world is likely to get the Benz.

———————————

In bad times, government seems to just keep rolling along, but many private companies run out of steam and go belly up. For example, we went on a tour to a perfume factory. When we got there, there was a sign on the door 'CLOSED. OUT OF ODOR'. I checked up on the company and sure enough, they didn't have a scent. They were bankrupt. They didn't have enough money to fix up the plant. It was an olfactory.

———————————

Working hard with a purposeful goal is healthy and often rewarding. An employee came back to his desk to eat his lunch and remarked to those of us in ear shot, "I worked all day this morning".

———————————

Joe delivered sand and gravel for a brick walk that I was constructing. I remarked to him that I had worked so hard my shovel was worn thin. He said that in his career he had worn many shovels thin. I then answered back, "But Joe, I just bought this new shovel last week".

After many complaints from the customers, a dry cleaner put up a sign 'IF IT'S GONNA, IT WILL , IF IT ISN'T, IT AIN'T'. Don't think this will stain his reputation.

Hands-on management sometimes has too many fingers in the pie.

Definition of Figurehead: Chief Financial Officer. Go figure.

Posthumous credits at the end of a western movie under the heading 'Stunt Men' read, "The late Joe Smith, the just too late Dick Jones and the almost on time, Harry Johnson". Proves that some jobs are more dangerous than others, especially when timing is critical to survival.

Not long ago, there was an audition in New York City for an actor to replace Christopher Reeves (Superman) who had passed away. A young, good looking Jewish man was certain to get the part until he read the lines 'Up, Up and Oy Vey'. He didn't get the job.

Labels that connote academic achievement such as PhD, Esquire, Reverend and Doctor warrant respect, but not trust or belief that their judgment is infallible. Respect the title, but realize that trust must be earned.

I worked for a company once with a large turnover. Those on break at the coffee machine would ask who's new instead of what's new.

In business, managers are often promoted in-house (from within). Apparently, they feel that in-house is better than outhouse.

At the age of 12, I negotiated to work in my grandfather's store. I asked him how much he going to pay me. He said that he would give me something far more important than money: Experience. I took the job. Besides experience, I also got a nice lunch. Can't beat that.

Mergers and acquisitions: A process where the company doing the acquiring is free to lay off workers while the management of the acquired company gets golden parachutes. That's capitalism at its worst. Union busting is another motivation.

In business, unlike the public sector, in good times the reward for outstanding achievement is continued employment. In bad times, forget about it.

Advertising: Lying by omission. Also, the science of deception.

To make money in the stock market, the first rule is never to trust your broker.

One archeologist on his colleague's theory: "Yes! I dig it".

Toward the end of the week in Zurich, the Clockmaker's Convention was winding down.

In good times, management throws money away. In bad times, they throw people away.

You will always get what you want because of your charm, your personality and your talent for blackmail.

The American manager of our Swiss-based company is a jolly fellow. He likes to ham it up at parties. When his Swiss counterpart is here for a visit, it's 'Ham and Swiss on a Roll'.

Sales and marketing is too often like sugar: empty calories, hype and promises.

Jack Benny, the comedian, was said to be so wealthy that he owned several banks which paid a high interest rate. I still would not put my money in his banks. I don't like to deal in funny money.

It should be wisely written that he who works just two days a week spends the first workday recovering from the long weekend and the other day daydreaming about the next one unless, of course, the boss is watching.

As Fagan ("Oliver Twist" by Charles Dickens) might have said to his boys off to pick pockets, "let's roll 'em".

When entering Walmart it helps to know Chinese. The employees won't understand you but the products will.

The infamous Mustang Ranch (whore house) has fallen on hard times lately. So much so that they're finding it difficult to make ends meet. It seems they're *barely* making a living. An investor has recently helped by putting some *skin* in the game. He owns a mattress company. Can't hurt.

Most people say that they remember faces, but names escape them. Bounty hunters, however, are likely to say that they know the names, but faces escape them.

"Everything is just fine. Just trust me". Have you heard this from: bank officers, real estate salesmen, stockbrokers, used car salesmen, doctors, politicians, salesmen in general, school administrators, lawyers, contractors, etc? Do you believe them?

Corporate parasites are those who feed off of the creativity of others and then attack their hosts by disposing of them after they're no longer needed. Whistle blowing is a difficult instrument to play, so the parasites almost always get away with it.

—————————————

Two jobs where you better not retire: Ponzi scheme operator and embezzler.

—————————————

Animals don't need economists. Why should we?

—————————————

Banking has replaced the oldest profession in reputation. Both are in the business of screwing the public.

—————————————

My course in economics at the university didn't start with a syllabus, it started with a stimulus package.

—————————————

Managers used to be dictators; now they do their own typing.

—————————————

What do you call a female chimney sweep? You call her a
flue-zie.

On a business trip to Dallas, a group of colleagues and I, intent on impressing the boss, went into a beer house after a day's work. With us was my Swiss counterpart, a beer expert. At the far end of the long table seating 18 of us, the waitress began taking beer orders starting with the boss. There were 76 brands available, mostly imports. When it came to our end of the table, opposite to that of the boss, I deferred to my Swiss expert, who with everyone silent anxious to hear his decision, answered "I vant a Budviser". I chimed in "Me too".

The more I call my broker, the broker I get.

One of the most profitable businesses in this country is insurance. They make money with fear. They get you to buy protection, similar to the old Mafia protection racket, by blowing risks way out of proportion. The main difference is that with insurance companies, if you don't buy their insurance, they don't make sure that you have a claim as the Mafia would do. Have you noticed how many ads on TV are insurance ads?

Insurance is like the lottery, except in the lottery, you pay to win and most often lose. In insurance, another law of the probability game, you pay hoping to lose and you most often don't. In either game, it is set up so that you don't win.

———————————

Trivia triumphs! Twitter twitches and *twembles*, spelling twilight time for the U.S. Industrial Revolution. What is left but re-runs? Easy access to information is nice, but if it doesn't enter the brain, it's useless. Frenetically force-feeding facts as food for thought may not encourage innovation as much as it adds to entertainment (the leisure industry).

———————————

I have supervision. I can always see my boss.

———————————

In chemical as in other research, I'm sure, it's nice to know chemistry or other, but it is essential to know what to do with it creatively to advance the art. Obvious? No, not to many in management. Managements are successful for reasons other than creativity. The ideal manager is one who also is creative, for example, the late Steve Jobs of Apple.

———————————

Many marketing mavens use mindless, meaningless metaphors for morons. They are money makers. What does that say about the average intelligence of people? The same public votes for our politicians who use the same tactics.

Writers, who use a lot of commas, may suffer from shortness of breath.

Oxymoron: Trusted attorney.

When asked what effect the recent natural disaster would have on the stock market, the stock broker being interviewed answered "Yes, we can make money from this disaster. I'm not a morality guy, I'm just a (stock) broker". True story. Can you believe it? This is a great example of amoral.

The board meeting was interrupted by a flasher. After the intruder was removed by security, the chairman remarked "Where were we before we were so lewdly interrupted?"

Business Person's Creed: Cents make dollars and dollars make sense.

Mafia policy: If you can't shake them down, shake them up.

Editor to writer: Your draft gave me a chill.

Islamic Economics: Instead of getting interest on bank loans, the bankers get a piece of the action (part of the company, a share of the business). Is this a good idea? Will this keep the banker bad guys in line? You don't hear that the Arabs are selling sub-prime mortgages for tent buyers or for trucking businesses (camel caravans).

In the U.S. today those are wealthy who have no mortgage, even though home prices have come down. The same holds true for a business. The business can not go bankrupt if it has no debt. If you have the money invested at higher return than you would get by paying off your mortgage plus the tax advantage, remember that you must continue to be aware of the risk.

Today, tablets are used for more than just writing the ten commandments. That is a good thing.

I do my searching on the subject of humor on 'Giggle' or 'Guffaw', but not on Google.

The insurance racket is the best idea the Mafia ever came up with. The archaic name was protection racket. They make money the easy way; they scare people into giving them money. Insurance companies never lose, ask someone from AIG (bailed out by taxpayers). Before medical insurance, doctors would make house calls and not charge a lot of money. Also, dentists didn't make a lot of money until the advent of dental insurance. Insurance is the business of fear.

Once we had spinning wheels that produced useful cloth products. Now we have spin doctors who cause us to wind down the wheels of progress.

"It's not so much how much you make, but what you do with it". This is the quote of a man who inherited nothing and claims never to have made more than ten dollars an hour in his sixty year lifetime. Yet he owns two houses and two cars in a middle class neighborhood in a small town. How did he accomplish this feat? He never overspent for anything. He stayed away from banks as much as he could. No mortgage or loans on a car. These are the two biggies that keep most people from getting ahead. He and his wife were good shoppers. He was a do-it-yourself person. All this with two children. Amazing. True story.

A battle cry in medieval times was to pillage the village or siege the city. This action was promoted by the king as a compensation to the marauders in lieu of salary.

Too many economists use sniffing glue to build their models of our economy. Consequently, their theories don't fly.

Efficiency is a private sector word.

No one poo poos the press like a bird in a cage. They often are the best newspaper critics. Too bad they can't critique computer articles.

Wall Street creed: Life, Liberty and the Pursuit of Greed.

Walking into the conference room just after a major company layoff, I noticed only about half the usual number of chairs was around the table. My colleague walking in behind me remarked "Gee, they even fired the chairs". True story.

A sign over a commercial garage reads 'RADIATOR UROLOGISTS - We Fix Leaky Radiators'.

Ditch Digger's Uniform: Trench coat

PART 11

Education

Far more precious than gold, a good teacher keeps our world from returning to the primitive life. A good teacher inspires students to continue on their own to enjoy one of life's most rewarding needs, the need to learn.

———————————————

On the other hand, a poor teacher will waste a student's precious time, keeping him or her from reaching their full potential.

———————————————

Aristotle once said that, to know how good your education is, know who your teacher's teacher was.

———————————————

It is, by far, too easy in most universities to get a degree in education, today. Recently a dean at a prestigious New York teacher's college belittled the value of a PhD in education in an op ed piece in The New York Times.

———————————————

In 2011, fifty per cent of teachers in the U.S. graduated in the bottom one-third of their class. No wonder we rank so low among the other developed nations of the world.

We must reverse the trend of inferior and mediocre education or our children and grandchildren will suffer a lower standard of living.

The majority of our college students is required to take remedial Math and / or English in their first year. By then their bad habits are set in stone.

The greatest harm to our education is not so much the teacher's union, but rather the administrator's union as well as gullible school boards and parents. These unions are not the first to destroy an industry. First there was steel, then rubber, plastics, chemicals and recently autos. However, it was the weakness of management that gave away the store during negotiations that really did the job.

The backbone of our country, free enterprise, is being seriously eroded by poor education and the lack of competitive products due to high labor costs.

Mark Twain said "God first made idiots and then he made school board members." Better boards would be a good start. Perhaps privatizing the schools should come next. Paying the company running the schools on the basis of student performance sounds great, allowing of course, for differences in neighborhoods,

When I was on a board of education years ago, an issue came up which is still apropos. The issue is whether school board members should be paid for doing good or should they be good for nothing. The way the system works now unfortunately results in many boards being good for nothing.

I'd like to ride on the learning curve. The view from the top must be awesome.

When considering the alarmingly high rate of teacher absences, it's obvious students need teachers who have more than just a 'touch of class'. Substitute teacher days are a waste of time for the students.

A school board member suggested good teachers be given a bonus. Another board member said it would cost too much. "Not in this system," the first replied.

Sports can be important in the life of some students. While sports are good for your scrapbook, academics are good for your pocketbook.

If the amount learned is in direct proportion to the time spent in the classroom, it's no wonder that U.S. students learn less than those in other developed nations.

Some schools of thought are schools for naught.

A century ago, an eighth grade education would prepare you for life. Then it was considered necessary to graduate from high school (where virtually everyone passes). Then a college education was considered necessary for a good future. Now some disciplines require a PhD. The education industry is not finished. Now children (ages 2 years 9 months to 5 years old) attend pre-school.

What has this accomplished?
- Kept millions of young people out of the job market.
- Provided millions of jobs for teachers and administrators.
- Has taken the pressure from elementary and high school teachers to provide a finished product.
- Students have learned a little more but apparently not enough to match those in the other thirty five plus developed countries of the world, at least in math and science.

Where do we go from here? Maybe the teachers or the administrator's union has the answer and are not saying. Their priorities are clear.

Some teachers give help; some teachers need help; and some teachers need help out the door. Unfortunately, with tenure, the last does not happen.

School renovation: Maintenance with an architect.

On a lighter note, my son and his classmates in kindergarten were visited by the first grade teacher who was sizing up her class for the coming semester. The kindergarten teacher reported that my son was a good boy and wouldn't be a problem. With that my son, looking up from his little chair, said "Yes, I like to be *teached*."

In too many school systems in the U.S. today, the purpose of education seems to guarantee teachers and administrators high salaries, excellent benefits and total job security rather than to prepare the students to get jobs that provide the same. It appears students are in school at the convenience of administrators and teachers. Thank goodness for those teachers who defy the system and "teach." Wish we had more of them.

Teaching to the test is good, if the teacher will make up a good test. At least you know some of what the students have learned by the results of the test. The problem is that it takes work for the teacher to make up a good test and time to grade it. Therefore simple tests requiring true or false or matching answers are given. Another benefit of testing is accountability of the teacher, administrator and the school itself. State tests were supposed to take the lack of accountability out of testing. In our state ,the union has found a way to dumb down the tests and the reporting of them. Nevertheless, tests may not be everything, but they are way ahead of what comes next.

One of the differences between my university and Yale is that the 'Keep Off The Grass' signs at Yale are in Latin. Is it true that at Harvard, their sign reads 'Don't Tread On Me'?

In college musical events, the number in the audience is in direct proportion to the number of students performing (mamas, papas, uncles and aunts), unfortunately not enough to fill the house.

In the 12th century, 95% of the people couldn't read. Today, 95% of the people won't read.

The late Albert Shanker, former head of The American Federation of Teachers said, "Today, if you're 18 and breathe, you can get into college." A corollary might go "Today, if you're 21 and breathe, you can graduate from college."

Because of the internet, libraries have more trouble with *under-do* (low circulation) than overdue books. Electronic books could turn libraries into museums.

Nonfiction adds to a student's learning. Fiction can confuse that learning. With most entertainment (fictional) that inundates us, it can be difficult to separate fact from fiction. Consider for example, how much fiction has crept into history books.

The less that you learn, the less you forget. Not funny when I overheard a teacher say "why bother teaching them, they only forget it anyway."

Historians are masters of hindsight.

Before learning comes yearning for learning.

Curriculum is subjective. What subjects turn you on?

Creativity does not depend on education; Effective creativity does.

A reader gets to live many lives; the illiterate is doomed to live just one.

My writing teacher said "when you write, you should write for your own consumption". A student asked "does that mean you should be prepared to eat your own words?"

In colonial Philadelphia on 6th Street there was the For All Tavern. The sign in front read, "King: I govern for all; General: I fight for all; Clergyman: I pray for all; Citizen: I pay for all." Clearly, the citizen is not getting their money's worth in education today. Education costs over the years have far exceeded inflation. How ironic, it seems, the more it costs, the less it's worth. Today our education costs almost twice as much as the second highest developed nation and with poorer outcomes.

Too many schools and universities are retirement homes for administrators and teachers.

At my University dining hall, cool, card-carrying kids can come to the catered cafeteria. The quality of the food is excellent. Unfortunately, junk food is still an option at each meal along with healthy foods.

Missing in many schools is a course analyzing truth in advertising. Students should learn early in life that deception is the rule and they should learn to be better consumers.

In business, there is no charity in the negotiation process. However, when boards of education negotiate with unions, charity dominates.

Teachers are more bigoted because they are so class conscious.

Math teacher's assignment for her class: "Go figure!"

Recipe for failure: If you don't know, don't ask!

"Today a college education may not amount to much, but at least you had a good time on your parent's money and you can at least say you finished something. Good luck in the future. You'll need it. You can always depend on entitlements and your parents for a living." Part of a commencement speech by Dr. Grouch.

Mark Twain said "Never let school interfere with your education." Thinking of school as a box, many times we learn more outside the box. At least don't expect too much from the box.

An effective teaching method is to give a formal lecture, allowing questions and giving spot quizzes from time to time followed by a comprehensive final exam. It's remarkable how few professors do this. Perhaps it's too much work. Also, A fifty minute final exam, down from formerly a three hour exam, says something about how much was expected to have been learned in the course.

In a science career you have the chance to make history. A history teacher can only talk about it. Who should be compensated more? Answer: the one who does the best job.

These days, almost as many people write books as read them.

Prepositions are taught last in grammar class. That is why prepositions are now used at the end of a sentence and that is where it is at. So there.

After auditing many courses at the local state university and hearing about many other universities throughout the country, I have come to the conclusion that they should no longer be considered institutions of higher learning. Instead rather, institutions of somewhat higher learning or, at best, merely extensions of high school.

Heard in economics class: "Today you must be in debt to create a good credit rating." How about saving money instead?

Mark Twain had a great grandson who wrote children's books. His name was Choo Choo (Twain). Sounds like another Twain that could and did.

Without school reform perhaps we should first focus on reform school for troubled teachers and administrators and start by taking away their tenure.

When you think about it, it really pays to study the so called dead languages, Latin and ancient Greek. After all, you will be dead for a long time.

Why are there so many squirrels on college campuses?
They love academia nuts.

True or false questions can be tricky. They should also allow for 'depends'.

One Board of Education member to another: "Just think. We can not be called cheap spending other people's money. What fun!"

Too many professors in this country believe that getting their PhD was their greatest accomplishment. The best ones do not rest on their orals.

The professor asked the class the definition of deterrent. One student answered "Isn't that what you put into your washing machine?" How did he get into college? I know. He had the money.

The problem with many non-fiction books is that their message could be much easier to comprehend in fewer pages. Unfortunately authors feel the need to embellish and expand the text so that it is long enough to warrant the classification as a book and not just an article or essay. Too bad.

Students, hungry to learn, in many universities in the U.S. are put on a starvation diet because many professors don't teach. Too many professors spend time in class assigning reading and will only discuss the assignment. What ever happened to lectures. Is the word becoming archaic?

Poetry is the art of using words in such a way as to eloquently express a thought often with rhyme. Unfortunately, too often words are forced in just to make them rhyme. Then you're supposed to look for the deeper meaning which is many times, a stretch. Lyrics in songs have the added dimension of music. Some are timeless, for example, 'Those were the days my friend, I thought they would never end'. How prophetic is that?

What we need in our school systems today is fewer uneducated educators.

Author's Creed: Never say in a word what you can make into a book. This is especially true for textbooks.

Do you know any one who has framed the gold star he or she got for perfect attendance in Sunday school? This has about the same value as earning an "A" at my university for some of the courses offered. I think they are still called snap courses. They do you no good but they make money for the university.

Students guilty of killing time pay the penalty without a trial but may get a life sentence.

In political science class you either *ism* or you ain't.

In political science, you talk about problems of the world. In science, you solve the problems of the world.

Common attitude of a tenured teacher: I get paid whether I work or not. The kids don't seem to mind. For them life is easier when I don't teach. Everybody wins. It only hits them later when they try to get a job. But by then they are long gone out of my classroom. Then it's their problem.

I am taking the course 'Philosophy of Happiness' at my university. Fortunately, I am auditing the course. Can you imagine, if I were taking it for credit and flunked the course, my transcript would always show that I flunked 'Happiness'. How catastrophic is that?

Debate: Where you trip over your tongue in rapid fire, a race to confuse the opposition. Where is the morality in that? Have you been to a college debate? Check it out.

Can tall tales fit into short stories?

Oxymoron: Well known ghost writers.

In our school system drop-out rates are low, but drop-in rates are high. Student attendance is mediocre. Too many seem to drop in when they feel like it, but they don't officially drop out of school. 80% of the drop-ins are poor students in our affluent district. What is the incentive? They know they will graduate and will be able to get into a college.

In the business of education, the product is learning. The quality and the quantity of learning, high or low, are often not recognized by the customer (the student). Unlike other products, in this case, you may learn too late you did not get your money's worth. Moral: Let the buyer beware.

After hearing the professor at my university suggest to the class that '9/11' was a President Bush conspiracy, I was inspired to write "Forget cholesterol, what may be more harmful to our nation's health are ACADEMIA NUTS."

PART 12

The Benediction (Religion)

Do we live on in the memories of others or in published evidence of our accomplishments only, or is there a life after death? Thinking is what we do to either rationalize or logically answer this question. So think about it. There are two schools of thought on this subject: theism and atheism.

Bottom line: Whether you believe or not, religion has done a good service over the centuries overall, because it has provided hope for a better life, created a structure in living, a major social good and stimulated music and the other arts. Hopefully, as science progresses, religion will adapt to the new world so the two can be more compatible in the future.

Atheists may think as follows:

- Cleanliness is next to Godliness, especially during brain washing.

- Ethnic cleansing is not next to Godliness.

- If it is true that the lottery is for those who flunked math, then does it follow that religion is for those who flunked science?

- Atheists believe that you is until you ain't.

- At church you are promised if you do right, you will go to heaven, but they don't put it in writing.

- To eliminate most war, replace religion with bingo and a few socials (picnics, etc).

- Religion has become simpler over time. For example, in ancient times when someone said to pray to God, you would have to ask "Which one?"

- If God is good, why have I got gout?

- In the atheist library, books on religion may be found in the section on fiction.

Revival meeting is a place to clear your mind of scientific facts and disturbing history of centuries of religious dogma that has resulted in the second biggest killer of mankind in human history (after mosquitoes).

There are many sects in all of the major religions of the world which evolved from squabbling on details, ultimately resulting in separation from the mother church. Not so with atheism. Atheists always agree with each other. Atheists do not go to war against each other.

Freedom of religion should include freedom from religion. How many public figures do you know who admit to being atheists? If they did admit it, they would never get elected to anything, no matter how honest and talented they were.

A skeptic believes that even so called facts are questionable. To the many skeptics past and future who have made and will make our lives better, I offer the coveted 'Doubting Thomas Award'. May they continue to persist? This works well in science, but is discouraged in religious thought.

Babies are innocent until proven guilty, although in some religions, they are believed to be born in sin. Try to make sense of that.

You have heard the expression 'having the patience of a saint'. It's easy for them, they are all dead. They haven't anything else to do.

Ever notice that there are no footnotes in the Bible?

K.I.N.G.: Kill In the Name of God. Take for example, the Crusades. It's a familiar theme throughout history.

The prayer plant does not respond to fertilizer for nourishment. The only way to make it grow is to feed it money from the collection plate.

In ancient times would-be prophets prognosticated the future based on the reading of cracks formed on animal bones after burning them. I wonder if the expression "It's not what it's cracked up to be" resulted from the failure of those prognostications.

I like a simple, practical religion. So that is why I joined the *Utilitarian* Church.

Most people get a friendly greeting of 'God bless you' when entering church. Not me. To me they say 'Heaven help you'. What did I do to deserve that?

Oxymoron: Real miracle. There is none. Call it a miracle if you don't have the knowledge to explain the event scientifically.

Politicians will say that all men are created equal, but one with an IQ of 60 and another with an IQ of 160 are not equal in my book. Also, the gene pool is flawed in that certain races are more prone to certain diseases. It seems to me like a major flaw in creation. Perhaps six days was not enough to do the job right.

Ever notice that Europe's cathedrals are filled with tourists and not parishioners. By latest count, only 11% of the natives go to church regularly. Why is that?

For millennia, organized religion provided the promise of hope for a better life after death because life on earth was generally poor. Now we have science which continues to improve our lives here on earth, allowing us to enjoy Heaven on earth.

Did Adam and Eve have navels? Why not? Oranges do.

Please don't debunk my fantasies with respect to religion. It helps me retain my sense of well being and hope for a better life.

In church you learn how to believe, but you do not learn how to think.

Will the person who lost a pearl necklace please form a line at the entrance to the church after the service.

When reason comes into play, dependence on faith will fade away.

Religious dogma must be administered early in life to endure throughout life. From time to time, booster shots may be required to keep the faith. At some point it must be separated from the belief in Santa Claus. Although neither has any basis in fact, both add to the interest in life, provide hope for good things to happen and keep the economy going.

When told to the Eskimos that Jesus could walk on water, one Eskimo replied "What's the big deal? We have been doing that forever."

Do you suppose they have comedy clubs in the Middle East?

Wouldn't life on earth be better if all religious dogma were put into the section on fiction in the library. Let clerics spend full time on social values and socials. This way they would be more inspired to make life better on earth than to preach that Heaven is the place for happiness. Without religious dogma, polarization from this source would disappear and lead to a more peaceful world.

Theopathy: Pathological theism.

Many adults are victims of their childhood teachings of religion. Once brainwashed, it is very difficult to later change their thinking out of loyalty to parents, church, friends and others.

"Rock of Ages": Antique jewelry.

Shepherds in the Bible were not stupid. After all, they did have sheepskins.

We hear in church 'to forgive us our debts and our debtors'. Does that mean our mortgage and our bankers? Well the government has already forgiven our bankers with taxpayer money. Should those taxpayers who did the right thing by not going overboard in debt pay for those who did? Does not sound fair to me.

Is harm-based morality instinctive in humans or must it be taught? If it must be taught, does enforcement of mores taught require fear of reprisal from the belief in an all-knowing God? Is life in our modern society without belief in God enough to hone the goodness of mankind? Has rule of law and interacting with our fellow humans for the common good been enough to keep us on the straight and narrow?

In developing your answers, keep in mind only the majority of people. There will always be outliers, a minority of humans who, because of genetics or other factors, are evil. Another consideration is 'The Divine Command Theory' which makes a case for the need of an all-powerful God. Theists and atheists will answer these questions differently. Where do you stand? Consider also the effects of rapidly developing scientific knowledge that dispel the myths found in the Bible, the Koran and other religious texts. The good in these texts is the guidance for living a peaceful, happy life. Many believe that God is not necessary to enforce morality.

Science is forging ahead, leaving religion in the dust.

15571615R00107

Made in the USA
Middletown, DE
14 November 2014